Bible Lessons for Techies

by

Valerie Poindexter Bennett, PhD

*Thriving in your Relationship
with God
Through a Technology Lens*

Supt. Whittley —
this book began with you! Thank you for believing in me and in the Robotics Ministry. Your leadership has meant everything to me. May God continue to bless you in all that you do!

Dr. Valerie Bennett

Copyright © 2017 by Valerie Bennett

All rights reserved. No part of this book may be reproduced in any manner without written permission except in the case of brief quotations included in critical articles and reviews. For information, please contact the author.

Cover Illustration Copyright © 2017 by Derek Nosa

Back Cover Photograph Copyright © 2017 by Antryl Warner

Dedication

This book is dedicated to several important people in my life. My parents, John and Lola Poindexter, are the lights of my life and teachers of all things wonderful. With the passing of my mom in 2012 and my oldest sister, Sheryl, in 2015, I felt that there was so much more that we had not done together, so I truly learned to understand that God's plans are not our plans. With my love and heartfelt gratitude for all that we did have the blessed opportunity to do, I dedicate this book to them. I also dedicate this book to my other incredible siblings, John, Cynthia, and Anthony who have supported me like no one else could ever do. You all are the absolute best and being the youngest of five, I have looked to you all to help lead the way.

To my best friend, loving husband, and scholar, Dr. Harold V. Bennett, who has been by my side through it all, your support and prayers are priceless. You have also been a great collaborator making sure lessons were hermeneutically sound and provided the best in Bible thinking and understandings. Lastly, I dedicate this book to my wonderful children, Quinton and Imani, who are bright lights that make the stars dim. I love you both dearly and thank you for all of the love and support you both have shown me.

About this Book

This series of Lessons is designed to enrich the spiritual lives of all people by using Technology as the lens through which we can read the Word. From the GPS, Virus Protectors and Programming, this book connects several Technology-based principles that give the reader insights into how those principles have a strong Biblical basis and the rich lessons they teach us about life. It's time to thrive in your relationship with God by studying the Word with new insights! Each engaging lesson contains a Brief Scriptural Background, A Techie Connection, Godly Principles, Reflection and Discussion Questions, as well as a Prayer for Growth and Connection. It also has Tips for Youth and Bible Study Leaders to guide them in how to use this book in their classes. Take the Tech Journey through the Bible!

Preface

Having been raised in a Baptist Church during my formative years and most recently part of a Pentecostal Church for nearly 30 years with a strong focus on the authority of the word of God, I have found many connections with how God works and how 'Tech' things work. Through the Word, I am growing in my understanding of God, and the Spirit of God has enlightened my thinking and enabled me to "marry", if you will, two areas near and dear to my heart - the teachings of Scripture and the logic of Technology. Being formally trained as a Mechanical Engineer and spending many years of my life gaining proficiency and knowledge in technology (and still growing and learning), and working with different youth groups in my Church and community, I could see even more connections between Science and Spirituality that my Pentecostal background and Spiritual understandings have afforded me.

The development of this project was birthed when I began to work with Scholastic Motivation Ministries in The Church of God in Christ. I wanted to bring something about the Bible to my work with teaching robotics to kids. In my search for finding that "something" to help kids make Biblical connections to some type of lesson with robotics, the answer was not at all immediate, direct, or apparent.

After thinking back over the many Robotics competitions, comebacks, adversities and growth that I have witnessed in students and Robotics teams that I have watched, mentored and coached, I knew that the Lord had given me a wealth of experiences to draw upon that would connect with many of the comebacks, adversities and growth through many of the individuals in the Bible. Although the starting point for these understandings grew out of my work with Robots, many of the lessons are an extension of several other fascinating concepts in the Technology world. I now share them with you.

Finally, being fully aware of the changing space and face of technology, a person reading this book perhaps two to ten years from now may find the connections "outdated" per se. The evolving nature of technology still relies upon fundamental principles that do not change so it is my intention to provide the starting point of connecting the fundamentals with the current discourse of the day. The Techie Connections with Biblical principles given provide similar insights to those parables that connect agriculture and farming with Biblical principles. I offer simply a technology lens.

Table of Contents

Forward................................viii

How to Use this Book......................xi

Lessons

Lesson 1...................................1
What will you Be?

Lesson 2...................................7
Did you Hear That?

Lesson 3..................................12
Follow the Program

Lesson 4..................................18
Decisions, Decisions

Lesson 5..................................25
Do More with Less

Lesson 6..................................32
Protect and Defend

Lesson 7..................................41
It is Clean Now

Lesson 8. 47
Who is your GPS?

Lesson 9. 53
I see it now

Lesson 10. 60
$\sum_{i=1}^{n} BOC(n) = 1$

Tips for Youth and Bible Study Leaders. 67

References. 70

Forward

I met Valerie Bennett while judging robotics competitions. She was the Teacher/Advisor for the team and had an in-depth knowledge of STEM. Valerie eventually became a judge. We've participated in several robotics competitions together and found that both of us had deep beliefs and phenomenal gifts in the world of STEM (Science, Technology, Engineering and Math).

Science and the Bible

When was the last time you read a PRACTICAL discussion about the Bible through the eyes of science/math/technology? So many view science and the Bible as mutually exclusive topics. In this study, Valerie Bennett gives a unique perspective on how those of us in the techie world can embrace the bible with our techie minds. I am an aerospace engineer and also a student of the bible. I've taken a few theology courses and, so far, cannot find a contradiction between the bible and science. When we believe that God created EVERYTHING; that includes the "science and math" we understand today to help us define the universe -- God's Creation. Without gravity, the scientific description on how we stay grounded on earth, we would all be floating around. How would we ever have a connection to our resources and other people? Have we stopped discovering our scientific explanations? Personally, I believe we have only begun to discover the "science" of the Universe and the bible is rich in information to explore God's Creation.

The bible is not a scientific discussion of God's creation. Yet, the bible has technical logic embedded within. Take the story of creation. God created the universe in a logical progression. For each day, God created what was needed for the next day of creation to survive. By the time God created on the 6th day, God already created all that humans needed to survive and thrive. God gives each of us gifts and expects us to use these gifts. We are the hands by which God expects us to carry out God's work in our Universe. If God's plan was for us to stay in the cave, God probably would not give us an inquisitive mind to study and understand how the universe works; that is, the knowledge to use math and science to define how our universe works.

This study gives a unique and needed dialogue that connects God and God's creation of Science and Math. The study shows us that our gifts of technology are relevant, not in opposition with faith. Science and faith work together that provides insight into the intricacies of the Universe, and how to use math and science to sustain our resources and replenish the earth for all. This study just scratches the surface of the Bible Lessons for Techies that relate to the technology world. Hopefully, it will be the stepping-stone for more Techie studies of the Bible.

As you work each of these studies, read the passages in the full context of the passage. Read the before and after passages of the wonderful stories given to us --- The People of God.

Karen Albrecht
Engineering Executive Lockheed Martin (retired)

How to Use this Book

This series of Lessons is designed to enrich the spiritual lives of all people, irrespective of background, age, stage, or geography. To my "Techies" – those individuals like myself who tend to be inclined to use technology as a lens for looking at the world – this book is especially for you. As an educator in the Private and Public High school as well as a having been a college professor in the areas of Engineering and Physics for nearly 15 years, I have come to realize that Godly principles and life lessons are truly all around us even in the world of Science, Technology, Engineering and Mathematics. The Lord has placed upon my heart to share these Godly principles and life lessons that He has shared with me in a series of Lessons and devotionals.

These lessons can be used in several ways. First, they can be used for kids in STEM programs to show how the Bible and Technology are connected. Youth Leaders can show kids through the scripture and discussion questions how what they are doing when they are building their robot, drone, bridge or coding their app relates to principles that God wants us to adopt.

Second, they can be used by Youth in churches as Bible study lessons. The students may be further engaged in the lesson by talking about technology in a church setting. They may initially feel that the worlds are separate, but these lessons will bridge the gap and enable them to feel more of a connection with the Word knowing that God truly IS in everything.

Third, adults can use the lessons to have conversations and engage their own young people and teenagers or with any persons who are true Techies of any age and stage. They can also serve as a witnessing tool to open up conversations about God, Jesus, and the Holy Ghost in relevant and interesting Bible lessons in the home.

Lastly, as you read through and experience each lesson, you may find other creative ways to use the lessons to help our youth grow in wisdom and knowledge. Our young people are extremely talented and gifted. This book is what God has given me as a way to make sure that their talents and understandings of how their technology lens can be used for a deeper understanding of His Word. This book utilizes the New International Version of the Bible in its references to scripture.

Lesson 1:
What will you Be?
God is Shaping me into what He wants me to Be:
I'm on the Potter's Wheel
Focus Scriptures: Jeremiah 18:1-6

This is the word that came to Jeremiah from the LORD: **²** "Go down to the potter's house, and there I will give you my message." **³** So I went down to the potter's house, and I saw him working at the wheel. **⁴** But the pot he was shaping from the clay was marred in his hands; so the potter formed it into another pot, shaping it as seemed best to him. **⁵** Then the word of the LORD came to me. **⁶** He said, "Can I not do with you, Israel, as this potter does?" declares the Lord. "Like clay in the hand of the potter, so are you in my hand, Israel."

Brief Scriptural Background

This scripture recalls a vision that God gave to Jeremiah. Our text constitutes a warning and a plea from God to Judah. The warning is that continued faithlessness will bring disaster, but faithfulness will bring prosperity. God chose to disclose this revelation through a familiar aspect of life in those times—pottery.

In the ancient world, pottery was everywhere. People used clay jars for storage and cooking, clay tiles for roofs, clay bricks to line their ovens, clay figurines for decoration and even for toys. The potter, therefore, was one of the most important craftspeople in the community. God is giving Jeremiah a lesson that he can share with the people of Israel so that when the people saw clay vessels, they would be reminded of the lesson.

There were two kinds of potter's wheels—one known as a slow wheel and the other known as a fast wheel. The fast wheel has a large circular stone parallel to the ground near the potter's feet and a small circular stone, rather like a circular tabletop, near the potter's hands. A vertical shaft connected the two stones. The potter would push the large bottom stone with his feet, causing it to rotate, and the top stone, connected by a shaft to the large stone, would rotate at the same speed. [1]

The genius of such a system is that the heavy bottom stone serves as a flywheel, smoothing the motion of both stones. If the potter were working with two lightweight stones, the spinning motion would be jerky. However, the heavy bottom stone adds momentum, causing the wheel to spin in a smooth motion. It would be much more difficult to make attractive pottery without that smooth motion.

As Jeremiah watches, the potter determines that the clay on the potter's wheel is unsatisfactory so he reworks the clay into another vessel. We do not know what the defect was, why the potter chose to rework it or how long the potter worked on the original vessel. The vessel must be reworked until it has a smooth consistency. He might need to add water to make it more pliable or add clay to give it more structure.

The potter does not simply throw the imperfect piece away, which is certainly an option. Rather, the potter begins what initially is a destructive process but it is really a creative process. Just as the potter turned the imperfect vessel back into a lump of clay and began again to fashion a usable vessel, so will God do with the people of Israel. He wants to create a new and faithful people out of the old and sinful people.

The Techie Connection

Getting a brand new Robotics Kit is so exciting. It is full of shiny and untouched parts that are just waiting to be made into something wonderful. I can even remember receiving a set of Tinker Toys as a little girl. My mind would race, imagining the endless possibilities that I could make, take apart, and then make something else.

When we get our Robotics Kit, the parts are sitting there with no ability to self-direct themselves to form into any functioning unit. The parts cannot spontaneously "jump" together and form themselves into a car, tank, or any other of the myriad of objects that they can possibly be assembled. The components sit in the box purposeless, with no direction, no opinion, and no form. The parts are essentially clay in our hands. What power we possess!

As we put the parts together, perhaps it is smooth sailing on the very first time we put the robot together. What I have found, however, that perhaps 3-4 minutes into the forming or building process, I see a more efficient and elegant way of putting the parts together. Perhaps not a complete redesign, but certainly an improvement on what I initially had in mind. As I get near the end, the design may still not be just what I had purposed to build so I may just make my last modifications right before putting it down to admire my handiwork. Suppose the parts had a totally different opinion of what they wanted to be formed into? Imagine as we are forming our robot into a particular shape or purpose, the parts revolted and fought with us (the Designers) all along the way, refusing to be placed in one particular place or another. How long would THAT build actually take?

Godly Principles

Realize God is the Ultimate Designer

Techies, realize that we are the clay, the parts in God's most capable hands. Unlike the parts in the kit, we have the ability to ask God what is His for us. The beauty of having a relationship with God is that we can ask the Designer what He wants our lives or into what

He plans to make us. Up to this point in our lives we may have an inkling of what His purpose is for our lives. We should get fully acquainted with His purpose through prayer so that we can allow God to shape us more and more into His ultimate, beautiful creation.

Realize God is the Ultimate Re-Designer

Remember how we were building that robot and had to make the improvement and adjustment in the design to make it even better than our initial design? Did not we feel compelled to make that change even when we needed to take a few parts off to make the changes that were necessary? Did not we just HAVE to put the absolute best robot out there? God is the same way with us. He wants the absolute best for us as well. When He sees that He must make changes in and through us to bring about His Perfect Will (Romans 12:2), He must do a re-design. Are we currently God's Version 3.01? What does it take to be malleable to God's re-design - whether small change or complete design overhaul? It takes an open heart and a listening Spirit during prayer. In God's own way, He will reveal to us what we must do to go in a changed direction or in a completely new direction. Remember, we are the clay on the potter's wheel, and we must be open to be formed and re-formed.

Reflection and Discussion Questions

What was the last thing you made or built?
Can clay mold itself?
If you could change one thing about your favorite toy, game or app, what would it be?
What type of person do you think God is making you into?
Is there such a thing as a perfect vessel?
What if we COULD make ourselves instead of allowing God to make us?
If you have kids, have your tried to "mold" them?
What methods did you use in trying to mold them?
Did your "molding" remain or did the clay (your child) undo the molding?

Prayer for Growth and Connection

Use the following words to guide you during your time of prayer:
To the Living God, who is the Creator of all things, I thank you for allowing me to be on your potter's wheel. Mold me as you see fit and touch my mind, soul, and Spirit to let me know that it is you, Lord, to whom I must yield. Show me Lord, even today, how I can become more of what you would have me to be. I am clay in your hands, Lord. In the name of Jesus, I pray. Amen.

Lesson 2:
Did you Hear That?
"Hearing the Voice of Jesus"
Focus Scriptures: John 10:3-5,27

³ The gatekeeper opens the gate for him, and the sheep listen to his voice. He calls his own sheep by name and leads them out. ⁴ When he has brought out all his own, he goes on ahead of them, and his sheep follow him because they know his voice. ⁵ But they will never follow a stranger; in fact, they will run away from him because they do not recognize a stranger's voice."
²⁷ My sheep listen to my voice; I know them, and they follow me.

Brief Scriptural Background:

In the Gospel of John, Jesus often uses illustrations, so that it might be easier to understand the lesson he is trying to convey. John 10:3-5,27 is a conversation Jesus is having with the scribes as to why people are following Him and leaning towards his way of thinking. He is in fact letting the scribes know He has followers, who he plans to build into disciples. To put across this point, he uses a very familiar example of sheep and a shepherd.

Sheep and their shepherds have a very special relationship.² There are a few requirements that make this relationship work. First, sheep must trust their shepherds. Next, shepherds must know each of his sheep. Finally, after a period of familiarity, connection, and trust between the sheep and the shepherd, the sheep only will follow the shepherd's voice and no others. In verse 5, Jesus says the following: a sheep will not follow the voice of a stranger but will instead flee from that stranger because the voice of the stranger is neither familiar nor feels safe.

The Techie Connection

This Techie Connection brings us to the concept of hearing, sensing and detection. Having the ability to hear or pick up on an instruction that is sent is quite an interesting idea when it comes to mechanical objects. Several components must all operate in order for inanimate objects to hear or sense a signal. A signal or "sound" must be sent out to an object by a transmitter on a particular frequency or range of frequencies. This signal is sent and must travel through some type of medium (air, vacuum, water, or a solid) and get to its destination without interruption, scrambling or misdirection. The object must have a receiver to accept the message that was sent. The receiver must then translate the message into a language that the object can understand and carry out the instructions.

Signals that are sent out or transmitted must be received at what are called resonant frequencies. A resonant frequency is a frequency at which it is easiest to get an object to vibrate or respond. For example, when we tune our radios to 102.5FM, we have just aligned a resonant frequency in the radio with a resonant frequency that has been transmitted, so we can receive only the 102.5FM signal.

Godly Principles

God has given us what we need to Hear Him

One wonderful thing about having a relationship with God is that He gives us what we need to have a great relationship with Him. We are His sheep so we need to follow His instructions. Although the sheep have ears to hear many voices, they zero in on the voice of the Shepherd. Like sheep, God has blessed us with even more tools/receivers to hear His voice. God has given us the Holy Ghost, our Comforter, Guide and Counselor. We can hear God's voice clearly because we have the key component, i.e. the Holy Ghost our "Spiritual Receiver," who can receive His messages.

God is sending signals at our Resonant Frequency

There are thousands of frequencies that are literally floating around us all of the time. The reason that we cannot hear or sense them is that we do not have the ability to tune in to pick up those signals. The wonderful thing about God is that He can reach us, because the Holy Spirit is set on the frequencies on which the signals are transmitted– the resonant frequency. God knows how to get our attention. We must make sure we are paying attention to the messages the Holy Spirit sends us. We must allow the Holy Spirit to guide us and be open to God's messages throughout the day. We must intentionally tune our Spirits to receive God's messages through prayer time because there is too much at stake for us not to be fully tuned-in to what our Designer and Creator is saying to us.

What I have experienced in my life the times when I have sensed that God has sent me a message is that I can literally feel vibrations, perceptions, as the Bible calls it, in my Spirit that He is sending an important message. We can recognize that it is a resonant frequency because the signal or message is so compelling that it cannot be denied. We are His sheep and we know His voice by the undeniable, irrefutable sense we feel deep down in our Spirit.

God's messages align with Scriptures

The Bible is, in a sense, a built-in fail-safe that we can count on, because if we are not sure of the message we are receiving or how to interpret the message, we can simply see if it aligns with what the Word of God says. We can check the Scriptures for assurance and reassurance. Knowing the scriptures helps us to verify the voice of God and avoid making spiritual mistakes. Matthew 22:29 says: "ye do err, not knowing the Scriptures nor the power of God."

Reflection and Discussion Questions

Who are His sheep?
What are ways that Jesus speaks to you?
What does His voice sound like?
When have you heard His voice?
How did you know it was the voice of God?
What was the result of that situation when you heard His voice, then you obeyed His voice?
What was the result of that situation when you heard His voice, and you DID NOT obey His voice?

Prayer for Growth and Connection

Use the following words to guide you during your time of prayer:
My Lord, you have given me so much. I thank you that in your graciousness, you have given me the gift of the Holy Spirit to enable me to hear your voice. Incline my ears, heart and spirit today, Lord, that I will be sensitive to the messages you are sending to me even now. Thank you, God, for helping me discern and filter out the messages that are not from you. I pray today for your Godly guidance. In Jesus' name, Amen.

Lesson 3:
Follow the Program
The Program is your Purpose
Focus Scriptures: John 10:3-5,27

³ The gatekeeper opens the gate for him, and the sheep listen to his voice. He calls his own sheep by name and leads them out. ⁴ When he has brought out all his own, he goes on ahead of them, and his sheep follow him because they know his voice. ⁵ But they will never follow a stranger; in fact, they will run away from him because they do not recognize a stranger's voice."
²⁷ My sheep listen to my voice; I know them, and they follow me.

Brief Scriptural Background

John 10:3-5,27 is the same scripture that was used in the previous lesson. The focus, now, however, turns to the part of the Scripture that has to do with the sheep trusting the shepherd and the sheep actually following the instructions the shepherd gives them. What is truly exciting about the shepherd-sheep relationship described in John 10:3-5 is that the shepherd calls each sheep by name and knows each one of them. Imagine a shepherd knowing the names of all the sheep and goats in his flock, as well as their personalities, strengths, weaknesses, and tendencies. Wow. What a caregiver.

Jesus talks about how shepherds call and lead the flock on a particular journey or pathway. The shepherd's instructions are given with authority - sometimes subtle - but direct. The shepherd's movement, movement of the staff, and the sounds all provide the sheep with the needed instructions to take the sheep where they need to go. Shepherds use clicking sounds; whistles of various tones and loudness are additional methods that shepherds use to communicate instructions to the flock. The sheep, in a sense, can almost NOT follow the instructions because they have developed such a strong relationship with the shepherd.

The Techie Connection

Sheep following the direction of the shepherd brings us to the concept of programming. Whether it is a program we are writing for an app, robot, or drone, or any device, the principle is the same – provide a set of detailed instructions to a platform upon which an entity can read the instructions and carry out those instructions. If you want to make the entity move, stop, blink, or make a sound, a clear set of instructions written in a language that the entity can understand is required. A robot, drone or app will only follow the instructions that are given. If the device is not responding as we thought, there was an error in the program. When I have written programs, I particularly enjoyed the debugging phase where I could find my errors in the program, make the changes, and see if the new instructions are followed perfectly.

We are similar to Robots – designed, built and given a program to follow, but with one difference: unlike Robots, we have "free will." We have heard the program or instructions, but along the way, the execution or carrying out the instructions somehow gets lost in translation. You see, we have "free will" and we have the choice to de-rail and re-direct God's downloaded program into something He never intended. Following the program somehow becomes optional in our eyes.

Something that must also be considered is that He may have given us a particular program to follow, but He needs for us to upgrade and so that He can update our software. Since we were not plugged into the source in prayer, we may have missed some critical updates that were necessary to operate at peak performance. What we are doing in life seems ineffective and unproductive.

Here's a scenario for us to consider: we have downloaded the latest version of software on our computer or phone only to find that the previous work we have done may not run anymore. Clearly there is a breakdown in the communication between the two entities. The new program is now trying to work with an old program and now they are incompatible. This is a situation where new wine is placed in old wineskins (Mark 2:22). This happened to me where I have used a new revelation from God with an old set of skills, ideas and beliefs to carry it out. God was calling me to do a new thing, but it required me to grow and change in a certain area. Be willing to do what is necessary for the program to work in your life.

Godly Principles

God's Program brings us to His Purpose

God giving us the program to follow is truly a blessing. It is not simply a set of instructions to be taken lightly but a window on His purpose for our lives. These instructions are certainly God's way of letting us know the how, when, and where. We should not in any way, compare or envy someone else's program. What God has for us is for us and hijacking someone else's program will only delay what God's wants to manifest in us.

God's Program provides comfort and solace

There is rest and peace in following God's program. There is simply no room in God's program for worry and angst that comes from facing unknown situations.

Philippians 1:6 says "Being confident of this, that he who began a good work in you will carry it on to completion until the day of Christ Jesus." The 'good work' is the program and purpose that God places in us. He is committed to bringing it to fruition so we should take on the peace of God as we follow His purpose for our lives. More assurance comes from Exodus 33:14, which says the following: The Lord replied, "My Presence will go with you, and I will give you rest."

Reflection and Discussion Questions

Do you know God's purpose for your life?
Was there a time that you followed God's program and purpose?
Have you ever been a leader and if so, what group did you lead?
Did your group follow your instructions? Why or Why not?
Were your instructions clear?
Did everyone in the group know the overall goal or purpose?
Did they follow you willingly or did they have their own opinions about how they should be led?
Was the overall goal achieved?
What would you have done differently, if anything, in your leadership role?

Prayer for Growth and Connection

Use the following words to guide you during your time of prayer:
My God, how excellent and wonderful it is to have your Guidance. Your instructions are true and meant to fulfill the purpose you have set before me. Thank you, God, for loving me so much that you will embed your purpose in me. Order my steps today and allow me to rest in your will. In Jesus' name, Amen.

Lesson 4:
Decisions, Decisions
Focus Scriptures:
1 Corinthians 13:11; Hebrews 5:12-14

1 Corinthians 13:11
When I was a child, I talked like a child, I thought like a child, I reasoned like a child. When I became a man, I put the ways of childhood behind me.

Hebrews 5:12-14
[12] In fact, though by this time you ought to be teachers, you need someone to teach you the elementary truths of God's word all over again. You need milk, not solid food! [13] Anyone who lives on milk, being still an infant, is not acquainted with the teaching about righteousness. [14] But solid food is for the mature, who by constant use have trained themselves to distinguish good from evil.

Brief Scriptural Background

In 1 Corinthians 13:11 and Hebrews 5:12-14, the writer makes references to persons who have heard the Word and know the work of Jesus. Persons who have started out on the journey with Jesus are referred to as babes who drink milk. These passages of scripture suggest that a correlation is present between how our thoughts and actions can be childlike, that is, without maturity and growth. This period in our lives is filled with indecision, doubt and mistakes. If we do not grow to point where we can understand the harder and more challenging mysteries of the Word of God, we end up making bad decisions because our spiritual growth has not caught up with the trials and complex circumstances we are facing.

1 Corinthians 13:11 takes our understanding of growth further. The author indicates that when he was a child, he spake as a child, but when he grew up, he put away childish things. Paul is fervent in his efforts to convince the Saints in Corinth that they must not be pulled into petty arguments and talked out of the truths that they have been taught. Hebrews 5:14 identifies wonderfully who can and should consume meat: "But solid food is for the mature, who by constant use have trained themselves to distinguish good from evil." The strong meat is meant for those who are mature to use their senses to discern, disseminate, rightly divide morally between good and evil. These persons can distinguish good and evil and have no room for the gray areas because ultimately they are prepared to decide issues.

The Techie Connection

Decisions, decisions, decisions. In the movie, *The Matrix*, Morpheus asks Neo which pill he wants to ingest: the blue pill or the red pill? Decisions, decisions, decisions For this installment of The Techie Connection, we return to our programming scenario but extend the scenario into the next level of programming – the use of conditionals or *if-then* types of statements. This phase is more intuitive and requires the application of logic in decision making for our electronic devices. Gone are the days of programming for simple movements and turns. The use of conditional statements in programs serves the purpose of decisions based on a predetermined set of conditions. These decisions respond to progressively more challenging situations wherein the robot must choose to go in one or another direction.

    This requires the programmer to be able to anticipate the different situations under which the device will find itself. When the object is ever faced with any of these situations, the program must be robust enough to handle each situation. For example, an ultrasonic sensor that can detect distance can be programmed to change direction or turn if the sensor detects that the robot is within a certain distance of a barrier. In the movement of the object we have programmed, we may not know exactly when it would encounter a boundary. We, however, do know as a programmer that whenever it DOES encounter a boundary, the object should move according to what was prescribed. God grows us up in Him by giving us progressively more challenging situations wherein we must choose to go in one direction or the other.

Godly Principles

God Provides you with conditional statements to help you make Godly decisions.

Romans 6:23 states that "For the wages of sin is death, but the gift of God is eternal life in Christ Jesus our Lord." In other words, God has provided us with the meat to be able to make Godly decisions – whether to turn left, right or simply to stop. The meat of the Word nurtures the wisdom and sensitivity to what is going on in a situation and casts light on how to handle it. This one scripture alone gives us a strong and powerful logic/conditional statement that makes it quite clear as to the consequences of our decision-making.

The equations are quite simple:

Sin = Death
vs.
No sin = Gift of God of Eternal Life through Jesus

In terms of a Conditional or Logic Statements:

```
if (decision = sin)
     death
else
gift of God of Eternal Life through
Jesus
```

```
do {
gift of God = Eternal Life through
Jesus;
} while (decisions = sin-free);
```

God's logic may be illogical to others

When we are faced with decisions in life and make up in our minds and Spirit that we will make a Godly decision, we need to realize that those around us may not embrace our decision. It may even be downright Illogical to them. They may even try to talk us out of it.

Faith can be one of the most illogical concepts to non-believers but it is perfectly logical to us as believers. Hebrews 11:1 teaches that faith is the substance of things hoped for; faith is the evidence of things not seen. This is one of the beautiful things about faith. Faith takes over where logic and reasoning may end. Is every move of God illogical? Of course not, but we must be open to the fact that some of His requests for us may be illogical, for God has told us that His thoughts are not our thoughts, and His ways are not our ways (Isaiah 55:8). Because of our flesh or sinful nature, it is difficult to receive or act on the things of God. When we become born-again and are in the will and purpose of God's program, we can gain confidence in His plans for us, and by following His plan for us, decision-making becomes easier.

Reflection and Discussion Questions

When have you been faced with a tough decision?
How did you finally decide which direction to take?
What were some of the circumstances, which influenced your decision?
What were all of the options?
Would God be pleased with that decision?
What were the logical and illogical choices?

Prayer for Growth and Connection

Use the following words to guide you during your time of prayer:

Dear God, how I praise you for all that you are and all that you have done in my life! For the decisions that are before me today, provide me with the Godly wisdom to make the choices that would be pleasing to you and done according to your will. I realize that your thoughts are not my thoughts, and that your ways are not my ways, but I can receive them in the Spirit. Help me today to be more mindful of your thoughts and ways in the Spirit. In Jesus' name, Amen.

Lesson 5:
Do More with Less
Focus Scriptures: Judges 6,7 (Story of Gideon)
Key Verses: Judges 6:12, 16; 7:2-4,7, 22

Judges 6:12, 16

¹² When the angel of the LORD appeared to Gideon, he said, "The Lord is with you, mighty warrior."

¹⁶ The Lord answered, "I will be with you, and you will strike down all the Midianites, leaving none alive."

Judges 7:2-4, 7, 22

² The Lord said to Gideon, "You have too many men. I cannot deliver Midian into their hands, or Israel would boast against me, 'My own strength has saved me.' ³ Now announce to the army, 'Anyone who trembles with fear may turn back and leave Mount Gilead.'" So twenty-two thousand men left, while ten thousand remained.

⁴ But the Lord said to Gideon, "There are still too many men. Take them down to the water, and I will thin them out for you there. If I say, 'This one shall go with you,' he shall go; but if I say, 'This one shall not go with you,' he shall not go."

⁷ The Lord said to Gideon, "With the three hundred men that lapped I will save you and give the Midianites into your hands. Let all the others go home."

[22] When the three hundred trumpets sounded, the Lord caused the men throughout the camp to turn on each other with their swords. The army fled to Beth Shittah toward Zererah as far as the border of Abel Meholah near Tabbath.

Brief Scriptural Background

Gideon was youngest son of Joash of the Abiezrites, a family who lived at Ophrah.[3] He was the fifth recorded judge of Israel. In the book of Judges, "judges" were local tribal leaders who were given specific tasks in regards to helping tribes in Israel gain deliverance from their enemies. When the angel appeared, Gideon was threshing wheat with a flail in the wine-press to conceal it from the predatory tyrants. Clothed by the Spirit of God, he blew a trumpet, and was joined by Zebulun, Naphtali and Asher. Strengthened by signs from God, he reduced his army of 32,000 to 300. Gideon's army would face the Midianites whose army has been reported to be between 120,000 and 135,000. Gideon was seemingly at a very unfair disadvantage. With Gideon's army of only 300, God instructed him to launch an attack.

Their midnight surprise attack upon the Midianites was something that can be described as tactics right out of the guerilla warfare handbook. They blew trumpets, smashed pitchers and caused so much disorder, that the terror-stricken Midianites were put into dire confusion. In the darkness, the Midianites ended up slaying one another, so that only about 15,000 of their great army escaped alive.

The Techie Connection

There are two Techie Connections that will be shared for this lesson – The Engineering Design Process and Tech Competitions. Doing everything with little is often the name of the game in Engineering. Producing the most efficient, durable, cost effective, and elegant solution is considered a major accomplishment. An elegant design is not necessarily the most visually beautiful (although that would be an added bonus); however, when something is well-designed, it refers to a solution solves the problem wonderfully and simply. It is incredible how great the solution is! Steve Jobs, former Apple CEO and Pioneer, would demand his team to make his products smaller and better. In other words, do more with less.   With advances in technology, there is the constant challenge to increase disk space and processing speed on a smaller footprint of the circuit board.

The steps of the Engineering Design Process have the overall goal of leading persons to such a solution. The typical steps are: Identify the Problem, Research and Brainstorm Possible Solutions, Select the Best Solution, Build a Prototype and Test, Improve the

Prototype and Rebuild, Present the Results. Now imagine Refining the Prototype and Rebuilding for several iterations until the most elegant solution is obtained. No problem, of course, if you had infinite time and infinite resources. The allotted time and resources available are dictated by those who need the solution. Regardless of the company or individual who may need the solution, I assure you that they would not be happy with a less efficient and hard to operate final product. In addition, the time and resources allotted are often not adequate for what is asked. To make it lighter, more efficient and to use the K.I.S.S. (Keep It Simple Students) Rule can be a Herculean task, even for the most experienced engineer. Somehow the job is done. You have achieved doing less with more and the end product is quite the marvel!

Science Olympiad, all levels of FIRST Robotics (Lego League, Tech Challenge and FIRST Robotics Competition), as well as so many other Tech Competitions have elements of 'solve this impossible task with very little time and resources'. Oh yes, by the way, make the solution innovative and elegant at the same time. Typically, 2-3 months are given to a team to prepare for these types of competitions. As a former Tech competition coach (and later judge), there is rarely a situation that has been ideal when we have been given a task to solve.

We have faced manpower and financial challenges. From team members being novice builders and programmers, to experienced members becoming sick the day of competition, it has been a continuous test of doing more with less. Reductions in budgets, speeding freezes, and financial constraints have also been some situations that our team had to face. Again, operating with less to do more. What we found was that God blessed us through all of those setbacks. There have been competitions where I was judging that team members may have left the team for one reason or another, members who could not attend, or situations when their robot simply stopped working for no explainable reason, computers crashed, hard drives were fried, you name it, I've seen it. The wonderful thing is that I have also seen teams rise to the occasion, and find that even when they have had less, they had more because they found innovative ways to simply use what they had and make it work.

Godly Principles

God is bigger than your Herculean task

Impossible situations are God's specialty, even when He orchestrates them, as in Gideon's case. No task or situation is too big or too great for Him to handle. As we look at the mountain ahead, we must look to the hills from whence cometh our help, because our help comes from the Lord (Psalms 121:1-2). The faith it takes to look up is what God is calling us to do. Trust and know that He is bigger, Bigger, and yes, BIGGER than whatever situation you are facing.

God wants you to grow in the process of you allowing Him to win the battle for you

Since we are now positioned to feast on the Meat of the Word, it requires that we face situations that are not easy for us to navigate on our own. These situations imply that we don't know all of the answers; however, they "demonstrate our faith."

Reflection and Discussion Questions

How do you think Gideon felt as God kept reducing his army?
What battles have your faced lately?
How did you know when God was taking away your army when you were about to go into a battle?
When have you been in a seemingly impossible situation?
What did God do and how did you respond?
Did your response delay or advance God's move in your life?
What was the outcome and what was your reaction?

Prayer for Growth and Connection

Use the following words to guide you during your time of prayer:

Dear God, help my unbelief! You are higher than anything than I can ever ask, think or believe so I think big and bold today about your possibilities for the situations I face today. You are a God who can do all things, up and above all that I can ask or think. In Jesus' name. Amen.

Lesson 6:
Protect and Defend
Focus Scriptures: Exodus 12:3,7,11-12; Psalm 23:5

Exodus 12:3,7,11-12

³ Tell the whole community of Israel that on the tenth day of this month each man is to take a lamb for his family, one for each household.

⁷ Then they are to take some of the blood and put it on the sides and tops of the doorframes of the houses where they eat the lambs.

¹¹ This is how you are to eat it: with your cloak tucked into your belt, your sandals on your feet and your staff in your hand. Eat it in haste; it is the Lord's Passover.

¹² "On that same night I will pass through Egypt and strike down every firstborn of both people and animals, and I will bring judgment on all the gods of Egypt. I am the Lord.

Psalm 23:5

⁵ You prepare a table before me in the presence of my enemies. You anoint my head with oil; my cup overflows.

Brief Scriptural Background

Exodus 12:3,7,11-12 is the narrative about the Passover. The Passover is the 10th plague that God sent through Egypt is His last attempt at getting Pharaoh's attention to let the Hebrews go and be under the new leadership of Moses. The lamb's blood was to be smeared on the two doorposts and on the beam above the doors in the homes of the Hebrews. If the blood was not there, the death angel would slay the eldest child in that home. Since Pharaoh's home was not protected in this way, Pharaoh's son was struck by the death angel.

In Psalms 23, David speaks about his relationship with God, and he uses his experience as a shepherd in talking about this relationship. In David's youth, he tended sheep and did all of the necessary duties of a Shepherd. He uses this experience to illustrate how God relates to him and to all those who are followers of God.

In verse 5, David talks about what God did to him – God anointed his head with oil. This is a particularly interesting statement, for perhaps David had in mind those times he anointed the heads of his sheep while they were in the field. The shepherd wants to provide the sheep with protection against flies, mosquitos, lice and ticks, which like to attack the eyes and ears of the sheep, and the shepherd would use oil to ward off these insects and keep them from laying eggs and infecting the sheep.[4] Disease or even the death of sheep would result if the sheep were not adequately protected against or left untreated from the infections done by such parasites. Sometimes a lamb suffers from being exposed to the intense rays of the sun, or its body may have been badly scratched by some thorn or bush. The most common remedy the shepherd uses is olive oil, a supply of which he carries in a ram's horn, because the shepherd is always on the lookout for members of his flock that need personal attention.

David compares the care and concern he has for his sheep to how God cared for and anointed him. In 1 Samuel 16:13, Samuel anointed David as a boy indicating that he would be King of Israel and that he was authorized and empowered to carry-out this office. It is important to note that the verse goes further to say that the Spirit of the LORD came upon David from that day forward. Just as the anointing was meant to protect the sheep from the parasites and all entities that would infect or weaken the sheep, so does God's anointing work in David's life to endow him with whatever he needs to be a successful King and representative of God.

Most notably is David's defeat of Goliath, a giant, soon after being anointed. Goliath was an enemy, a parasite, to the nation of Israel. Previous defenders of Israel failed to defeat this worthy opponent. Yet David, with a mere slingshot and a handful of stones, defeated Goliath with the power of God's anointing resting on his life.

The Techie Connection

I wonder if this has happened to you. You are surfing the Internet and while you are typing to complete a task, you get a warning, "You have hit a FIREWALL" and searching must end. This can be quite frustrating especially when you are in the midst of completing an important task. A firewall is a program or hardware device that filters the information coming through the Internet connection into your private network or computer system.[5] If the filters "flag" incoming information, the information is not allowed to enter your computer. Without a firewall in place, your computer becomes vulnerable to potential hackers who could put viruses, make FTP (File Transfer Protocol) connections to other computers, and wreak havoc on any computers that may be networked to your computer as well. These internal computer locks enable the computer to determine what information is allowed to enter and what is to be discarded. A break in the security system allows for hackers to take advantage and weaken the strength of an otherwise well-functioning company or personal computer. The news has reported of how customer information may be compromised due to hackers finding ways to circumvent computer security firewalls that were put in place.

God has provided two spiritual firewalls (or spiritual locks) to protect us from the hand of the enemy. First, The Blood of Jesus is applied to our lives. "The Blood" brings attention to the sacrificial work of Jesus, by bringing attention to how it places us back into a correct relationship with God. When we accept Christ into our lives and believe that Jesus died for our sins, this confession activates "The Blood" and it, then, bring us back into the right relationship with God (Hebrews 9:22).

Second, the anointing firewall is a physical, external manifestation of an inward power we receive when we receive the Holy Ghost. Acts 1:8 says: "But you shall receive power when the Holy Spirit comes upon you; and you shall be my witnesses both in Jerusalem, and in Judea and Samaria even to the remotest parts of the earth." The anointing is there for us to move in the area of influence that God has given us. It, too, equips us to be successful in our "spiritual callings." Yes, the anointing commissions us for specific jobs, and it is waiting in us to be developed. The Blood of Jesus and the anointing of the Holy Spirit - what a 1-2 punch for the enemy!

Godly Principles

God wants us to receive His Spiritual Protection

Just as the shepherds anoint the head of the sheep with oil so they will not succumb to the flies, pests, and parasites, God anoints our lives to protect us from the hand of the enemy that comes to devastate our lives. The enemy can come in many forms—both big and small – and can attempt to come through our ears (what we hear), eyes (what we see), nose (what we smell or inhale), and the goal is to take over and devastate our lives. How wonderful it is when the Shepherd anoints the sheep and, how wonderful is it when God anoints us. Two ways we develop this anointing and abide under this covering is by staying in God's presence in prayer time and by maintaining a close relationship with God. It is important that we stay near the source of the protection to receive that divine protection.

God's protection is not meant to isolate us

Are the sheep then anointed to stay in the barn to never face the elements? Certainly not! Even Jesus says in Mathew 28:19-20, [19] Therefore go and make disciples of all nations, baptizing them in the name of the Father and of the Son and of the Holy Spirit,[20] and teaching them to obey everything I have commanded you. And surely I am with you always, to the very end of the age.

God's anointing enables us to move in our calling and to face and repel those fiery darts that we will indeed face as we move in this world. God does not offer us protection just to have us sit in isolation and do nothing with the gifts He has given us. Rather, we are to go forward in the midst of these challenges with our firewall filters securely in place—the spiritual protective coverings of the Blood of Jesus and the anointing of the Holy Spirit. Our firewalls will be challenged by various situations and events in the form of parasitic people, thoughts, music, beliefs, business deals, books, or foods. Keep in mind, however, we are not in a fight against people but against spiritual wickedness (Ephesians 6:12). The anointing of God protected David tremendously, for it protected him against the 14 attempts on his life by Saul.[6]

God wants us to remain protected but we must stay connected

To keep the sheep protected, shepherds would anoint his sheep more than once. As the oil slowly wears off or is rubbed off in the midst of the movement of the sheep and, because of his concern for the wellbeing of the sheep, the shepherd will re-anoint the heads of the sheep. Similarly, God wants us to remain anointed and protected. That is why we must ask in prayer for God's anointing and protection to remain in our lives. We are forever dependent upon God for all things. David was anointed three times; (a) by Samuel in David father's house, (1 Samuel 16:13; (b) when the tribe of Judah accepted and enthroned him as their king, (2 Samuel

2:4); and (c) when David was about 30 years old when he began his reign as king (2 Samuel 5:1-5). He was king for 40 years.

Reflection and Discussion Questions

When was the last time you encountered some type of Firewall when you were using your computer or other system?
Why do you think the Firewall was there?
Have you been anointed by God? How do you know for sure?
Are you protected by the Blood of Jesus? How do you know for sure?
What types of things do you think God is protecting you from?
Have you faced any fiery darts lately and were they deflected from touching you?
Have you been anointed by God more than once? How did you know?

Prayer for Growth and Connection

Use the following words to guide you during your time of prayer:
Dear God, thank you for the protection of the Blood, and for the anointing of the Holy Spirit and for how both divinely protects me from things seen and

unseen. As I walk into this new day, I ask that you continue to protect my heart, mind, and spirit. Anoint me again, Lord, as you would have me to move in the calling for which you have placed upon my heart.
In Jesus' name, Amen.

Lesson 7:
It's Clean Now
Focus Scripture: Isaiah 1:16

Wash and make yourselves clean.
Take your evil deeds out of my sight; stop doing wrong.

Brief Scriptural Background

Isaiah is admonishing the people that in order to be right before God, the sacrifices they were making were not turning the mind of God towards them in a favorable way. Their legal purification rituals and ceremonial washings fell far short of what God required. Instead, their sacrifices were only seen as an outward showing rather than a true repenting heart. Instead of the mere outward things they were doing, Isaiah was God's voice to the people to impress upon them to remove the grime from their hearts.

The Techie Connection

One of the most frustrating things most of us have experienced when it comes to working on our computer is getting the indication that there is a virus on our computer. Most of the time, there are no direct indicators that anything is wrong. Week after week we use our computers and there is smooth sailing. Soon we notice that it is taking longer to reach our favorite websites. The homepage of our browser is different. Your computer then takes forever to open up the last file you just edited. Running our programs is now sluggish. If our computer is unstable and crashes fairly often, we may have a problem and if we try to access files but receive a message saying they are corrupted, it is too late because our computer is now infected or has been long infected with a virus. Our computer has been the victim of an attack.

Viruses, worms or malware includes applications that spy on what we do on our computer, corrupt our data, destroy our hard drive or give control of our computer to someone thousands of miles away.[7] No matter what form it takes, it is bad business.

Scanning and removing malware from our computer is now essential for us to be able to access files. Cleaning our computer of the virus may not be such a simple process because tricky viruses often disguise themselves as seemingly safe installs on your computer.

Virus scanners and cleaners have a set of criteria that must be met in order for a file to be allowed to stay on our computer. If the file does not fit this stringent set of standards, the infected file or program is rejected. The best scanners and cleaners go far beyond a simple set of criteria. The operating system and other foundational files are checked such that a deep clean is completed. The best cleaners have the ability to even root out those mirrors files that "look" like they are good files, but are disguised as a real file we have created.

Don't be fooled. Second Corinthians 11:14 says that "And no wonder, for Satan himself masquerades as an angel of light." If we are not sure if we have been infected by a spiritual virus, Proverbs 6:16-19 gives us the criteria to check ourselves to see:

There are six things the Lord hates, seven that are detestable to him: haughty eyes, a lying tongue, hands that shed innocent blood, a heart that devises wicked schemes, feet that are quick to rush into evil, a false witness who pours out lies and a person who stirs up conflict in the community.

Rest assured: if we are doing any of these things, a spiritual virus has infected us. These spiritual viruses can be in the form of ungodly thoughts, jealousy, envy, gossip, and backbiting.

Godly Principles

God wants us to choose to want to be clean

Being cleansed from those spiritual viruses is a choice. It is comforting to know that we can choose to draw nearer to God at all times. It is even more wonderful and comforting to know that even when we slip and fall or when we have faltered in what God has called us to do, we have a pathway back to Him. We must choose to take that path. One of my favorite scriptures is Psalms 51:10; it says, "Create in me a pure heart, O God, and renew a steadfast spirit within me." This scripture gives me comfort and reassurance. We can reach out to God and ask Him to clean us when we acknowledge a spiritual virus has infected us.

God has given us everything to make sure we stay clean

God has given us the vehicle of repentance to clean and re-establish a right relationship with us after we have allowed the spiritual viruses to infect our lives. We must allow God to wash us through our willingness to renounce our wrong doings, thoughts, and actions, and commit ourselves to never doing them again. The scripture teaches: The person who covers his/her turpitudes shall never prosper, but the person who confesses and forsakes his/her wrongdoings shall obtain mercy (Proverbs 28:13). Repentance is an action on our part, that signifies to God our true heart's sacrifice or willingness to get rid of the filthiness of our flesh and spirit. This was the type of repentance for which Isaiah called. God requires it and He expects it from us. We are just not saying words that we are sorry just for the sake of saying them. We are 'fessing up as to the true nature of what has happened, and have made every possible effort to correct the situation, if the offense involved another person.

God's Word provides encouragement and motivation for us to repent. Ezekiel 18:30 which says, "Therefore, you Israelites, I will judge each of you according to your own ways, declares the Sovereign Lord. Repent! Turn away from all your offenses; then sin will not be your downfall. Acts 2:38 says, Peter replied, "Repent and be baptized, every one of you, in the name of Jesus Christ for the forgiveness of your sins. And you will receive the gift of the Holy Spirit." Still another is 1 John 1:9 which says "If we confess our sins, he is faithful and just and will forgive us our sins and purify us from all unrighteousness."

Reflection and Discussion Questions

Have you been affected with a virus that affected you physically (cold, flu)? What was the treatment and how did it cleanse you of the virus?
Have you been infected with a virus that affected you spiritually? What was the treatment and how did it cleanse you?
How did you know that you were infected with a spiritual virus?
What could be the danger if you left a physical and spiritual virus untreated?

What can you do to make sure you are least likely to be infected with a spiritual virus?

Prayer for Growth and Connection

Use the following words to guide you during your time of prayer:
Lord God, I ask that you forgive me for all ungodly thoughts, feelings of jealousy, envy, and gossip. I sincerely repent of all things that are not like you and things that are not pleasing to You. My prayer Lord is for you to create in me a clean heart, O God; and renew a right spirit within me. In Jesus' name. Amen.

Lesson 8:
Who is your GPS?
Focus Scripture: Exodus 13:21

By day the Lord went ahead of them in a pillar of cloud to guide them on their way and by night in a pillar of fire to give them light, so that they could travel by day or night.

Brief Scriptural Background

Exodus 13 begins with the Lord giving Moses instructions on sanctification and purification as they prepare to travel to the Promised Land. Moses and the Israelites must journey to the Promised Land, a Land that flows with milk and honey. Neither Moses nor the Israelites know exactly where the Promised Land is located; they only know that it is the land of the Canaanites, the Hittites, the Amorites, the Hivites, and the Jebusites. This land was promised to the Israelites' fathers so the Lord is fulfilling a promise that was made a while in the distant past. To get to the Promised Land, the Israelites, however, must rely on the guidance and leading of God to get there.

Throughout the Israelite's time in the desert, and as they traveled from Egypt to Canaan, God used the pillar of fire and a pillar of a cloud to lead them and to remind them of His presence. When the pillar of God moved forward (in the form of the cloud and fire), the people of Israel would pack up their camp and follow behind it. Similarly, when the pillar of God's presence stopped, the Israelites would set up camp underneath it. In fact, Lord's Tabernacle was set directly underneath the pillar of the cloud. This way, God's presence was always visible in the camp. The pillar of a cloud and pillar of fire were no doubt a holy and awesome manifestation among the people. Having such a powerful physical and visible symbol of God's presence gave them a source of reverence and safety.

The Techie Connection

Usually when we seek the help of a Global Positioning System (GPS), it is usually when we need to find our way. We initiate the communication with our phones or in-car navigation system. We rely on its instructions – turn by turn – to take us directly to our destination. We are often offered different routes to get to our destination, but nonetheless, we know that in the end we will get there. The GPS is truly an amazing technological advance that has simplified how to get from point A to point B, all without stopping at the gas station for directions. Initially developed for military navigation purposes, it is now widely used as a means of seemingly self-navigation.

What did we ever do before GPS? Generations of travelers before us have used other means to get where they needed to be. They have erected monuments, which served as physical landmarks. African slaves, who were seeking to escape the harsh realities of chattel slavery in America in the nineteenth century used stars and constellations to guide them to freedom. There have also been detailed maps. Many years ago, my husband and I would utilize the help of a driving company that would provide us with Driving Tickets, which were detailed step by step maps of each leg or segment of the journey. We would flip through each section of the map every few miles.

When we talk about a GPS, we mean that we have a GPS receiver in our possession – a smartphone or some type of on-board navigation system. GPS is actually a constellation of nearly 30 Earth-orbiting satellites circling the globe at about 12,000 miles per hour, making two complete rotations every day.

The receiver of the GPS locates four or more of these satellites, figures out the distance to each, and uses this information to deduce its own location. This operation is based on a simple mathematical principle called trilateration. Trilateration is a three-dimensional concept, but here is a simple two-dimensional example of how trilateration works.

Imagine you are somewhere in the United States and you are totally lost—for whatever reason—and you have absolutely no clue where you are. You can ask three trusted friends, "Where am I?" One of your friends says, you are 147 miles from Birmingham,

Alabama. This is helpful, but only a little, because you can be 147 miles from Birmingham in ANY direction radially away from Birmingham. You ask a second friend and they tell you are 214 miles from Columbia, SC. This narrows your location, but still, you can't precisely figure out where you are located. Your third friend tells you that you are 215 miles from Nashville, Tennessee. From these three reference locations, there can only be one place where they all intersect, Atlanta, Georgia. You finally know where you are located!

This same concept works in three-dimensional space, as well, but then you are dealing with spheres instead of circles, but the principle is the same. In summary, the GPS receiver has to know two things to find you: the location of at least three satellites above you and the distance between you and each of those satellites. For our Spiritual lives, trilateration is provided by the Trinity—Father, the Son, and the Holy Ghost—and gives us the GPS we need to navigate us to our purpose.

Godly Principles

The Trinity can tell us where we are Spiritually

First, the Father (God), the Son (Jesus) and the Holy Ghost define not only where we are spiritually, but who we are spiritually. The Trinity is a gauge or meter stick, and each person in this relationship plays a role in alerting us to our levels of spiritual maturation. It is important to know our location in the Spirit, so that we can be honest in our relationship with the one who created us.

The Trinity can tell us where we need to go spiritually

The Trinity also has the incredible supernatural ability to meet us in our spiritual locations and navigate and guide us to higher levels in God and into deeper understandings and of His will. Just like for our GPS in the natural, if it tells us to go left, we should go left. Sometimes, we may get creative to go right instead. The GPS is not flustered. It simply says, ". . . Rerouting." The GPS is determined to get us to our destination, just as the Trinity is determined to guide us and lead us to the will for our lives. Our cooperation and willingness to yield to the guidance is essential in getting us to the destination. The Trinity is there to navigate us through each situation because ultimately, the end destination is already calculated and calibrated for each of us. How wonderful it is to have access to the ultimate GPS! We simply must ask through prayer each day. The Trinity will never tire of our requests for guidance.

Reflection and Discussion Questions

Do you know where you are in God?
Do you know where God is leading you?
Have you ever gotten off course and how we are re-routed?
Have you ever needed to make a complete U-turn?
How safe (or uncomfortable) did you feel when God led you to uncharted territory?

Prayer for Growth and Connection

Use the following words to guide you during your time of prayer:

Dear God, I thank you for being my guide and leading me to do your will. Incline my heart, Spirit, ears, eyes and mind to you now that I may walk in the path you have chosen for me. Your Word is a lamp unto my feet and light unto my path. Open my understanding of your Word so that I may be able listen and follow your guidance. In Jesus' name. Amen.

Lesson 9:
I See It Now
Focus Scripture: Matthew 1:20

But after he had considered this, an angel of the Lord appeared to him in a dream and said, "Joseph son of David, do not be afraid to take Mary home as your wife, because what is conceived in her is from the Holy Spirit."

Brief Scriptural Background

Visions and dreams have a strong place in the Bible. There are many figures in the Bible who have experienced them—Jacob, Joseph, Isaiah, Ezekiel, and many others. In the "dream" and "vision" scriptures, the vision or dream was clear, undeniable, and provided an answer or information to the person who dreamed or experienced the vision.

One vision story comes to mind—Matthew 1:18 indicates that Joseph and Mary were husband and wife. Matthew 1:18, too, indicates that Mary was pregnant, but not by Joseph, her husband. Once Joseph learned of Mary's pregnancy, it was justifiable for him to feel tremendous angst because of the shame and disgrace such a condition created for the marriage. Imagine what he must have thought, knowing his wife had been intimate with another man. Adultery has always been considered a crime of a very heinous nature in the biblical community, for the punishment prescribed for it was death by stoning to the parties involved in the act (Leviticus 20:10; Deuteronomy 22:22; John 8:5).

    Think about how Joseph must have felt knowing that Mary was with child, but that she was not pregnant by him. Matthew 1:19 implies that Joseph was considering his options. It is important to note that this passage indicates that Joseph was a good man, and that he decided against making her a public example. Joseph chose to handle this horrible condition in a discrete and kind manner. He was unwilling to expose Mary to public ridicule, alienation, stigmatization by the community, or to death itself. Mary knew the backstory: she was aware that she got pregnant through the miracle of the Holy Ghost; yet Joseph, who loves Mary deeply, was trusting his common sense and was convinced something had gone awry. Herein comes the dream in Matthew 1:20.

    Through the dream, God gives Joseph the answer. God revealed the truth, i.e., what happened to Mary. Joseph had no more doubts about Mary's character; no more concerns about Mary's commitment to the marriage; no more questions about divorce. The dream provided a reliable answer to the question and situation with which Joseph struggled.

The Techie Connection

A Virtual Reality (VR) created environment is very much like a dream. Similar to the world in dreams, VR created reality goes far beyond computer simulations. VR literally recreates realness such that you cannot distinguish between the human world and the digital world. How is this done? It requires many components, each bringing an important part to make it all appear seamless, natural and real. A typical computer simulation of video game can be 2D or 3D in nature. The graphics and sounds may be amazing, but the experience, is nonetheless, distant and the line between the digital world and the real world cannot be crossed. The VR world, however, fully immerses the user in the environment such that the line between the digital world and real world is seamless and virtually undetectable. You feel one with this 3D world. You can also interact with this environment in meaningful ways. You can speak commands, they are followed, and you can virtually touch objects, which initiate additional actions or sequences. The combination of a sense of immersion and interactivity is called telepresence.[8] Computer scientist Jonathan Steuer defined it as "the extent to which one feels present in the mediated environment, rather than in the immediate physical environment."

A true VR experience causes you to become completely unaware of your real surroundings and focus on your existence inside the virtual environment. We now have all types of VR viewers and devices that can take your smart phone and transform videos that have been recorded with a special 3D camera into a VR experience for you.

But how is it possible for a digital world to emulate the human world? This must be done through stimulating your senses. Two of the five senses are engaged in most VR worlds. The display's resolution and the complexity of the environment's graphics (sight) are an initial step. This is done by creating a smaller, self-contained 3D environment, similar to what is created in your experience while watching a 3D movie.

A sophisticated sound system is another key component. If these two senses are engaged on an extremely high level, the other three senses (touch, smell and taste) are semi-suppressed because your brain is activated so highly with the other two senses. Many hand-held devices are slowly reaching the market to give VR users a sense of touch.

VR environments also have the power to trigger emotions because when the senses of sight and sound are stimulated, it also creates undeniable physiological or bodily responses. While experiencing things within a VR environment, users can experience changes in heart rate, changes in bodily temperature as well as sweating.

God creates a VR world for us in His use of dreams. God's dreams are vivid, clear in its message and align themselves with the Word of God. In Joseph's case, God used His voice to communicate vital information to address a specific problem Joseph was having in his life. I know that when I have had dreams, I awaken with a definite memory of the dream that spoke to a particular question I had. The clarity of the dream was breathtaking and the sounds and feelings of pure immersion made every moment real.

Godly Principles

Dreams can play a key role in the lives of those who love God.

God so wants to connect with us, and He will communicate with us in every way that He can reach us. God will use a dream to speak to us. God is also faithful to answer our prayers. Joseph had an extremely pressing issue that not only affected his life, but that of his wife and possibly his future child. We are important enough to God for Him to know the impact of dreams have on our lives. We may not remember our last lesson in school or the names of persons we met long ago, but a dream given by God stays with us. The answers God gives us in dreams creates long term memories within us because of the realism and voice in which God communicates to us. His answers cut to the core.

Dreams energize your faith

In the midst of situations that seem impossible to us, God may step in through dreams to provide us answers. This gives us hope and grows our trust in the Almighty God. How more are we assured than knowing that God Himself has spoken to us when we are most in need of an answer. Whenever we find ourselves in challenging life decisions, we can draw upon the fact that we have heard God speak and in anticipation, we expect that He can speak in and to this situation.

Reflection and Discussion Questions

How do you know a dream is from God?
When was your last dream you knew was from God?
What was the dream about?
Can you describe in great detail how you felt and what you thought when you awoke from your dream?
What senses (smell, taste, hearing, touch, sight) were activated during your dream?
Was your faith renewed after your dream?
Did the dream give you clarity of purpose?

Also, look at Genesis 40:8 and 1 Corinthians 2:10 for more insights into dreams and their impact on the dreamer. Tyler Wolfe's book, *The Christian's Dream Guide*, is another helpful resource to Christians and their Dreams.

Prayer for Growth and Connection

Use the following words to guide you during your time of prayer:
God of Heaven and Earth! How wonderful is your name! You are mighty and great in all that you do and all that you have done in my life. I thank you for listening to my prayers and requests in my time of struggle. I know you are able to speak to me in dreams. If you choose to reveal yourself in this manner, God, help me to be sensitive enough to hear your voice and understand all that you desire to reveal to me. Help me to understand the visions and dreams you are gracious to share with me. I thank you for choosing me to be one of yours. In Jesus' name. Amen.

Lesson 10:
$$\sum_{i=1}^{n} BOC(n) = 1$$
The Sum Equals to One
BOC stands for the Body of Christ
n represents all of the parts of the Body of Christ
Focus Scripture: Romans 12:4-5

[4] For just as each of us has one body with many members, and these members do not all have the same function, [5] so in Christ we, though many, form one body, and each member belongs to all the others.

Brief Scriptural Background

Paul speaks to individuals who have been recently converted. His goal here is to encourage those persons to see themselves as part of a larger Christian community. Paul wanted them to look at themselves as persons who are intimately connected to one another and to Jesus Christ and he used the body as an illustration. Christ is the "head" of the body while the "members" of the body are seen as members of the Church.

The Techie Connection

Having observed and worked with robots such as Sumo Bots that talk to each other to play a game as a team, it is quite clear that one bot could not possibly do all that is needed for the entire team. To enable different robots with different capabilities to communicate, collaborate, and act, is quite challenging and requires the use of Artificial Intelligence (AI). First, let us look at what AI is and how its ability to enable communication and action between robots brings us to our Techie Connection.

AI simply defined is the Science and Engineering of making machines or programs intelligent (the ability to achieve goals). AI is not a new concept. In fact, Alan Turing gave a lecture in 1947 exploring the concepts of AI. If we fast forward to IBM's *Watson*, which is a single AI computer capable of cognitive (reasoning) computing by the use of machine learning, it is clear that AI provides computers a pathway to human reasoning and thinking processes. To test *Watson's* capabilities and robustness, it was an actual contestant on Jeopardy and was placed in competition with the show's best and brightest contestants. Needless to say, *Watson*, hands down, won every match by huge margins.

How can machines or robots work as one? We can utilize the unique abilities of each machine computer or robot through constant machine-to-machine communication to make collaborative actions seamless. The individual tasks that several robots can do individually can be maximized for performance and work with the other robots efficiently and harmoniously. On a sports team or job, each member has a certain skill set. When each person utilizes his or her set of skills in a collaborative manner, phenomenal tasks and accomplishments can be achieved.

In the article, *Making Robots Talk to Each Other*, Sklar states that "Getting different types of robots to talk to each other and collaborate means each can focus on what it does best."[9] When we give two robots the ability to communicate in real-time, the possibilities for their teamwork are vast. Researchers at Carnegie Mellon University have done just that: enabled two robots with very different capabilities to collaborate to fulfill a request. One robot, Baxter, was a stationary robot, equipped with two arms that can delicately manipulate objects, while CoBot had no arms but was adept at navigating indoor spaces and could reliably deliver objects using its front-end basket. The researchers wanted each robot's strengths to make up for the other's shortcomings. The robots communicated wirelessly to provide feedback to each other, which allowed them to work together even when things didn't go exactly as planned.

In "Robots that Communicate with Each Other," swarm behavior, another type of collaboration between robots, is discussed.[10] Swarm behavior utilizes large collaborations of many robots modeled after insectile or animal behavior. In swarms, all the robots are built to complete the same task and use subtle cues from other robots to maximize the efficiency of the collective. This new collaborative robot model is also analogous to human teamwork. Robot collaboration can potentially eliminate the need for overly complex general robots, which are large investments and often more complex than needed.

This entire discussion about collaboration and working together naturally brings us to how we in the body of Christ are part of something bigger than ourselves. We need each other because as being part of the body of Christ, each of us plays a major role in carrying out God's will and purpose in this world. No one person or gift is deemed "greater" because that would be similar to saying that an arm is better than a leg.

Godly Principles

God gives each person gifts because each of us is an important member of His Team

God is so gracious and generous to freely give each of us specific gifts and talents, and God gives us these gifts because we are the physical extension of Christ in the earth. We are the body of Christ and members (1 Corinthians 12:27). Because we are the body of Christ, God gives each of us different spiritual gifts for the purpose of carrying out His will on the Earth and ensuring that the body functions effectively.

So, which spiritual gifts does God give to the believer? Several lists of gifts appear in the Bible. For the sake of manageability, I will mention just a few places where this subject receives treatment in the Bible. Romans 12:6-8 mentions exhortation, giving, leadership, mercy, prophecy, service, and teaching. First Corinthians 12:1-10 states that wisdom, knowledge, faith, the gifts of healing, the working of miracles, prophecy, tongues and other gifts. Another listing appears in Ephesians 4. This list mentions apostle, prophet, evangelist, pastor-teacher, Other inventories of gifts appear in the Bible, e.g., celibacy (1 Cor. 7:7,8), hospitality (1 Pet. 4:9,10), missionary (Eph. 3:6-8), and voluntary poverty (1 Cor. 13:3). Each part of the 'Christian body' has its place and we must know where and what our part is so that we can fulfill God's purpose for our lives.

God wants us to work together

Did you know that God needs you in order for Him to complete His work? You are important to God. God knows that individually we have gifts and talents but we are limited if we were to only work by ourselves. Our collective purpose allows us to have an even larger impact on the world if we work together without ego or pretentiousness. Each part of the body of Christ matters and none is deemed insignificant. Each of us has what it takes to make a difference on God's team.

Reflection and Discussion Questions

What gift or gifts has God given you?
How do you know for sure?
Have you ever used your gift(s)?
What was the response when you used the gift?
Can you recognize gifts in others?
How can you envision working with the gift God has placed in others to increase God's influence in people and in the world?

Prayer for Growth and Connection

Use the following words to guide you during your time of prayer:
Dear God, I thank you for making me a part of the body of Christ. You have placed within me gifts and talents and I ask you reveal all that you have placed inside of me for your purpose. How should I use them today? Show me how and who you would have me to work with for the purpose of advancing your Kingdom. In Jesus' name. Amen.

I also add this prayer that Paul provides that summarizes my hope and prayer for you:

We continually ask God to fill you with the knowledge of his will through all the wisdom and understanding that the Spirit gives, so that you may live a life worthy of the Lord and please him in every way: bearing fruit in every good work, growing in the knowledge of God (Col. 1:9-10)

Tips for Youth and Bible Study Leaders

1. Plan your Lesson
   - Review the Lesson before presenting it to your students
   - Determine which learning targets apply most appropriately to the age/grade level of students you are working with
   - Decide which discussion questions you find are most appropriate and engaging for your age group

2. Make the Lesson Fun and Engaging
   - If your class is working on a technology-related activity (Building, programming, competition), use a lesson that connects with what you are doing.
   - Gather all needed supplies BEFORE class. I suggest at least a few days before to alleviate the dreaded run to a store at 6am.
   - Ask yourself the question, "Would I want to come to my class?"

3. Get Assistance from Volunteers
   - Kids love helping kids and adults love to help other adults so get those wonderful expert helpers to help finish planned projects. Whatever the age or stage, make sure that they

have a passion and temperament for working with your group.
- Meet with volunteers prior to the lesson to provide them with instructions and guidance for what they need to do. Volunteers love to help, they just need to know what to do.

4. Assess their learning to make sure students have achieved your Learning Objectives
- What did you want them to know? Did you want them to remember the scripture? Did you want them to know more about the Techie Connection?
- How will you assess them? Will they need to provide a verbal or written answer? Is a group presentation needed? Do they have to build or make something?

5. Let others know the great things you have done in your class
- In accordance with the rules and regulations of your organization, make sure you follow the protocol. Do the parents have to sign a photo release? Make sure you ask someone in your organization who can answer this definitively for you before proceeding.
- Why Share? There are several reasons to do this:
  - To grow your program

- To touch the lives of even more young people
- To channel more resources to your program, i.e., volunteers, supplies, in-kind donations, finances

Here are some ideas for ways to share:

- 5 minutes during a service or conference
- Approved postings on social media
- Presentations to other youth organizations in and outside of your area

References

[1] https://www.sermonwriter.com/biblical-commentary/jeremiah-181-11

[2] https://www.sheepusa.org/IssuesPrograms_AnimalHealth_AnimalCareWelfare

[3] http://www.bible-history.com/smiths/G/Gideon/

[4] http://www.bible-history.com/

[5] http://computer.howstuffworks.com/firewall1.htm

[6] 1. Javelin throw (1 Sam. 18:11) 2. Javelin throw (1 Sam. 18:11) 3. Philistine battle to win Merab (1 Sam. 18:17) 4. Philistine raid to win Michal (1 Sam. 18:25, 27) 5. Saul's servants and sons Jonathan (1 Sam. 19:1) 6. Saul's third throw of the javelin (1 Sam. 19:10) 7. Messengers sent to David's house (1 Sam. 19:11) 8. Messengers sent to Naioth (1 Sam. 19:20) 9. Messengers sent to Naioth (1 Sam. 19:21) 10. Messengers sent to Naioth (1 Sam. 19:21) 11. Saul goes to Naioth (1 Sam. 19:23) 12. Saul's journey to the wilderness of Maon (1 Sam. 23:25) 13. Saul's journey to the wilderness of Engedi (1 Sam. 24:2) 14. Saul's journey to the wilderness of Ziph (1 Sam. 26:2)

[7] Jonathan Strickland "How to Remove a Computer Virus" 10 April 2009. HowStuffWorks.com. <http://electronics.howstuffworks.com/how-to-tech/how-to-remove-computer-virus.htm> 2 January 2017

[8] Jonathan Strickland "How Virtual Reality Works" 29 June 2007. HowStuffWorks.com.<http://electronics.howstuffworks.com/gadgets/other-gadgets/virtual-reality.htm> 8 January 2017

[9] https://www.technologyreview.com/s/539806/making-robots-talk-to-each-other/

[10] daily.jstor.org/robots-that-communicate-with-each-other/

Notes

Notes

Made in the USA
Columbia, SC
27 June 2017